BARCELONA

RESTAURANTS & MORE

BARCELONA

RESTAURANTS & MORE

Angelika Taschen

Photos Pep Escoda

TASCHEN

HONG KONG KÖLN LONDON LOS ANGELES MADRID PARIS TOKYO

El Raval

Barri Gòtic
El Born
La Ribera

La Barceloneta

L'Eixample
Gràcia
Tibidabo

Poble Sec
Sant Antoni

El Raval

Boadas

Carrer dels Tallers 1, 08002 Barcelona
☎ +34 93 318 88 26
Metro: L1, L3 Catalunya

Carmelitas

Carrer del Doctor Dou 1/Carrer del Carme 42
08001 Barcelona
☎ +34 93 412 46 84
www.carmelitas.biz
Metro: L3 Liceu

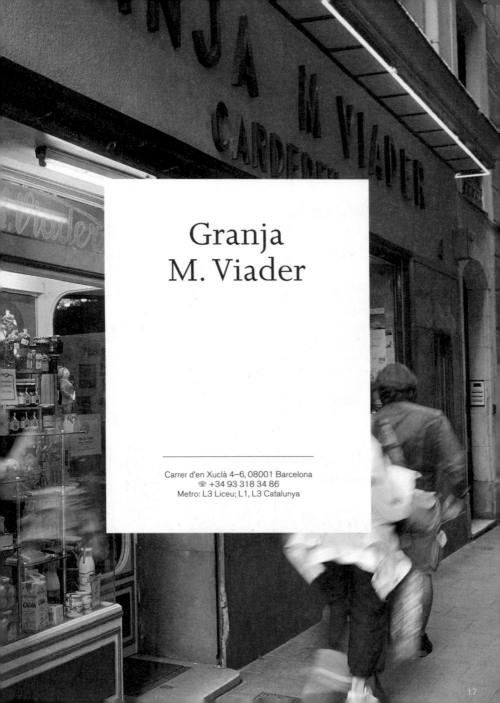

Granja
M. Viader

Carrer d'en Xuclà 4–6, 08001 Barcelona
☎ +34 93 318 34 86
Metro: L3 Liceu; L1, L3 Catalunya

A L'OBRADOR
D'AQUESTA GRANJA
L'ANY 1931
ES VA ELABORAR
PER PRIMERA VEGADA
EL CACAOLAT

V I A

GRANJA

M·VIADER

Granja M. Viader

Vaca "LINDA" 36 H

Padre: "ADEMA"   Madre: "CORONELA"

Producción   **4.439 l. - 171 Kg.** manteca en 300 dias

4.870 " - 192 " " en 383 dias

(5.º mes de gestación)

Según Control Oficial de la Junta P. de Fomento Pecuario, realizado
por los Servicios Técnicos de Agricultura de la Diputación Provincial.

Granja M. Viader

Vaca "METJE" 70 H

Producción
en 1.er parto   **4.743 l. - 192 Kg.** manteca en 300 dias

6.161 " - 255 " " en 433 dias

Producción actual 28'1 litros diarios en el 5.º mes.

Según Control Oficial de la Junta P. de Fomento Pecuario, realizado
por los Servicios Técnicos de Agricultura de la Diputación Provincial.

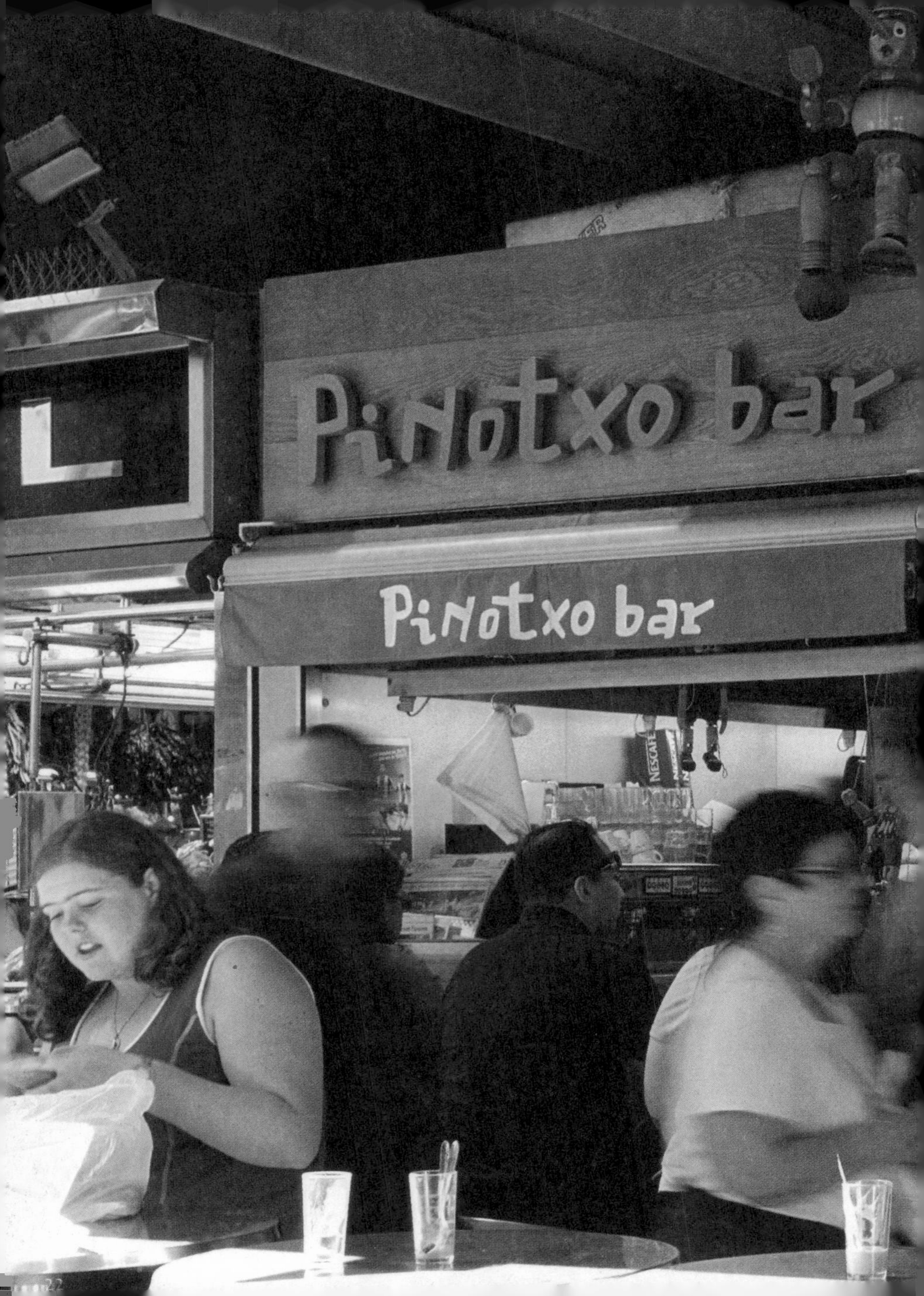
Pinotxo bar
Pinotxo bar
NESCAFE

Pinotxo Bar

Mercat de la Boqueria, Plaça de la Boqueria
La Rambla 85–89, 08001 Barcelona
☎ +34 93 317 17 31
Metro: L3 Liceu

Boadas

Carrer dels Tallers 1
08002 Barcelona
☎ +34 93 318 88 26

pp. 8/9

Classic Cocktail Bar
Interior: Unchanged since 1933

Open: Mo–Sa midday–2am | **X-Factor:** Charming owner María Dolores | **Prices:** Cocktails from 5 €.
Picasso, Miró und Dalí once sat in this tiny family-run bar – the black-and-white photographs on the walls tell of its many famous guests.

Öffnungszeiten: Mo–Sa 12–2 Uhr | **X-Faktor:** Die charmante Inhaberin María Dolores | **Preise:** Cocktails ab 5 €.
In dieser winzigen, familiengeführten Bar saßen schon Picasso, Miró und Dalí an der Bar – Schwarz-Weiß-Fotos an der Wand erzählen von den berühmten Gästen.

Horaires d'ouverture : Lun–Sam 12h–2h | **Le « petit plus » :** La charmante propriétaire María Dolores | **Prix :** Cocktails à partir de 5 € | Picasso, Miró et Dalí ont fréquenté eux aussi ce minuscule bar à l'ambiance familiale. Au mur on peut voir les photos en noir et blancs des illustres clients.

Carmelitas

Carrer del Doctor Dou 1
Carrer del Carme 42
08001 Barcelona
☎ +34 93 412 46 84
www.carmelitas.biz

pp. 12/13

Mediterranean Restaurant in a former Monastery
Design: Pilar Líbano

Open: Daily 1.30–4.00pm and 9.00pm–midnight (Th–Sa until 1am) | **X-Factor:** The vegetarian food | **Prices:** Meals from 4–21 €.
The head chef buys at the Boqueria market close by and creates his dishes with fresh seasonal ingredients.

Öffnungszeiten: Täglich 13.30–16 und 21–24 Uhr (Do–Sa bis 1 Uhr) | **X-Faktor:** Das vegetarische Angebot | **Preise:** Gerichte 4–21 €.
Der Chefkoch kauft auf dem nahen Boqueria-Markt ein und kreiert damit eine Karte aus frischen saisonalen Zutaten.

Horaires d'ouverture : Tous les jours 13h30–16h et 21h–24h (Jeu–Sam jusqu'à 1h) | **Le « petit plus » :** Les plats végétariens | **Prix :** Plats 4–21 € | Le chef fait ses courses au marché de la Boqueria tout proche et propose ainsi des mets d'une grande fraîcheur et variant au gré des saisons.

Granja M. Viader

Carrer d'en Xuclà 4–6
08001 Barcelona
☎ +34 93 318 34 86

pp. 16/17

Nostalgic Milk Bar
Interior: Original 1930s

Open: Mo 5–8.45pm; Tu–Sa 9am–1.45pm and 5–8.45pm | **X-Factor:** "Mel i mató" (cream cheese with honey) | **Prices:** Cacaolat from 1.25 € | Opened in 1870, their more than 20 milk-mixes are still served by waiters in white jackets: from the "orxata" (almond milk drink) to the "suizo" (cocoa with whipped cream).

Öffnungszeiten: Mo 17–20.45, Di–Sa 9–13.45 und 17–20.45 Uhr | **X-Faktor:** „Mel i mató" (Frischkäse mit Honig) | **Preise:** Cacaolat ab 1,25 € | 1870 eröffnet, über 20 Milchgetränke werden von Kellnern in weißen Jacken serviert: von einer „orxata" (Mandelmilch) bis zum „suizo" (Kakao mit Schlag).

Horaires d'ouverture : Lun 17h–20h45, Mar–Sam 9h–13h45 et 17h–20h45 | **Le « petit plus » :** « Mel i mató » (fromage blanc au miel) | **Prix :** Cacaolat à partir de 1,25 € | Depuis 1870, une vingtaine de boissons au lait sont servies par des serveurs en veste blanche.

Pinotxo Bar

Mercat de la Boqueria
Plaça de la Boqueria
La Rambla 85–89
08001 Barcelona
☎ +34 93 317 17 31

pp. 22/23

Vibrant Market Bar
Interior: At the heart of the covered market

Open: Mo–Sa 5.30am–5pm | **X-Factor:** A veritable institution | **Prices:** Meals from around 5 €.
The city's chefs-de-cuisine meet here for a "cortado" before going shopping at the Boqueria market.

Öffnungszeiten: Mo–Sa 5.30–17 Uhr | **X-Faktor:** Eine Institution | **Preise:** Gerichte um 5 €.
Früh am Morgen treffen sich die Küchenchefs der Stadt hier auf einen „cortado", ehe sie auf dem Boqueria-Markt einkaufen.

Horaires d'ouverture : Lun–Sam 5h30–17h | **Le « petit plus » :** Une institution | **Prix :** Plats env. 5 €.
Tôt le matin, les cuisiniers de la ville se rencontrent ici autour d'un « cortado », avant d'aller faire leur marché à la Boqueria.

Barri Gòtic
El Born
La Ribera

Granja
La Pallaresa

Avinguda de la Catedral

Plaça
d'Antoni
Maura

Avinguda de P

Carrer de la Palla

Carrer del Bisbe

Carrer de Mercaders

Cuin
Santa

Carrer de la Palla

Carrer dels Banys Nous

● Caelum

Carrer de Sant Sever

Pl.
Sant Ju
Café
d'Estin

Via Laietana

Carrer del Call

Carrer de la Llibreteria

Plaça de
l'Àngel

Ca

Plaça
de Sant
Jaume

Carrer de Jaume I

JAUME I

C. Vigatan

Plaça
de Sant
Miquel

Carrer d'Avinyó

Carrer de la Ciutat

Carrer de la Palma
de Sant Just

Carrer de l'Argenteria

C. Templers

Carrer del Sotstinent Navarro

Carrer del Regomir

La Vinya
del Senyor

Carrer d'Avinyó

Carrer d'en Carabassa

Carrer d'Angel
J. Baixeras

Passa
del I

Carrer dels Còdols

Carrer d'en Serra

Carrer d'en

Gignàs

Carrer de la Fusteria

Carrer d'en

Via Laietana

Carrer del C

Ample

Carrer

Carrer de la Mercè

Plaça
d'Antoni

Colom

Passeig d'l

La Torna

el Pellisser

ambó

Carrer d'en Grait

rina

Carrer d'en

Mundial Bar

Restaurant
Borràs
l'Econòmic

Plaça de
l'Acadèmia

Carrer dels Carders

Carrer d'en Tantarantana

Carrer del Comerç

Passeig de Pujades

Carrer dels Assaonadors

Santa Maria

la Princesa

Picasso

la Ciutadella

Carrer de Montcada

Carrer dels Flassaders

Carrer del Rec

Carrer de la Fusina

Bar
Gimlet

Carrer del Comerç

Carrer Comercial

Parc de

El Xampanyet

La Paradeta

dels Sombrerers

Passeig del Born

Carrer de
l'Esparteria

Carrer del Rec

Carrer de la Ribera

Passeig de

del Mar

Salero

de
a
ia

Pla de
Palau

Avinguda del Marquès de l'Argentera

Estació de França

Granja
La Pallaresa

Carrer de Petritxol 11, 08001 Barcelona
☎ +34 93 302 20 36
Metro: L3 Liceu; L1, L3 Catalunya

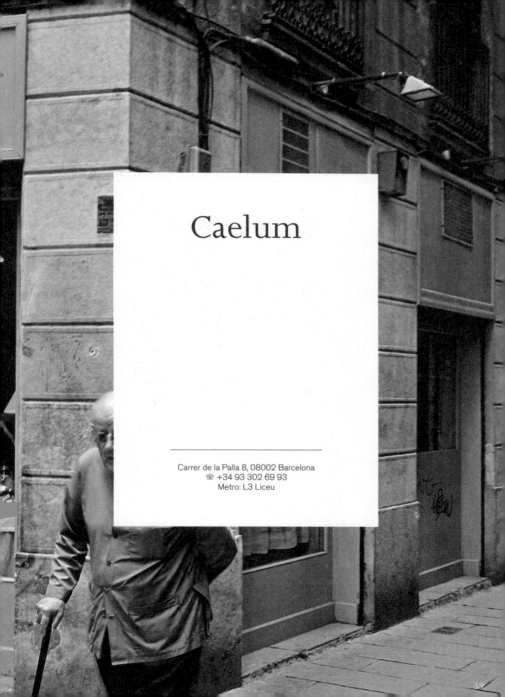

Caelum

Carrer de la Palla 8, 08002 Barcelona
☎ +34 93 302 69 93
Metro: L3 Liceu

Cafè d'Estiu

Plaça de Sant Iu 5–6, 08002 Barcelona
☎ +34 93 268 25 98
www.museumares.bcn.es, www.textilcafe.com
Metro: L4 Jaume I

La Torna

Mercat de Santa Caterina
Avinguda de Francesc Cambó 16, 08003 Barcelona
☎ +34 93 319 58 21
Metro: L4 Jaume I

Cuines
Santa Caterina

Mercat de Santa Caterina
Avinguda de Francesc Cambó 20, 08003 Barcelona
☎ +34 93 268 99 18
www.grupotragaluz.com
Metro: L4 Jaume I

Mundial Bar

Plaça de Sant Agustí Vell 1, 08003 Barcelona
☎ +34 93 319 90 56
Metro: L1 Arc de Triomf

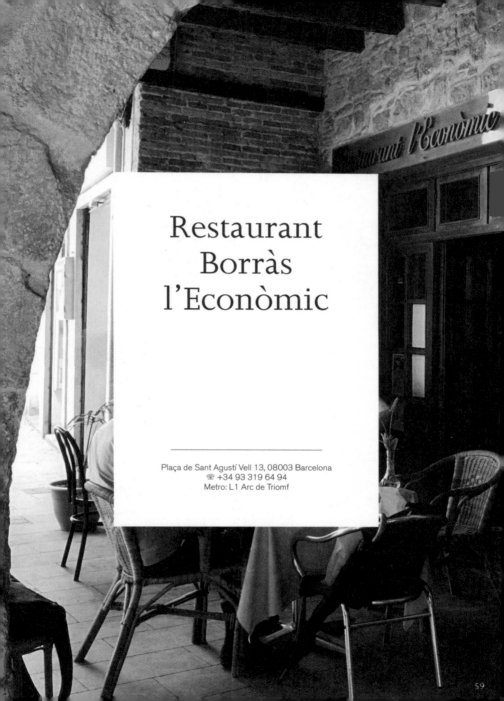

Restaurant Borràs l'Econòmic

Plaça de Sant Agustí Vell 13, 08003 Barcelona
☎ +34 93 319 64 94
Metro: L1 Arc de Triomf

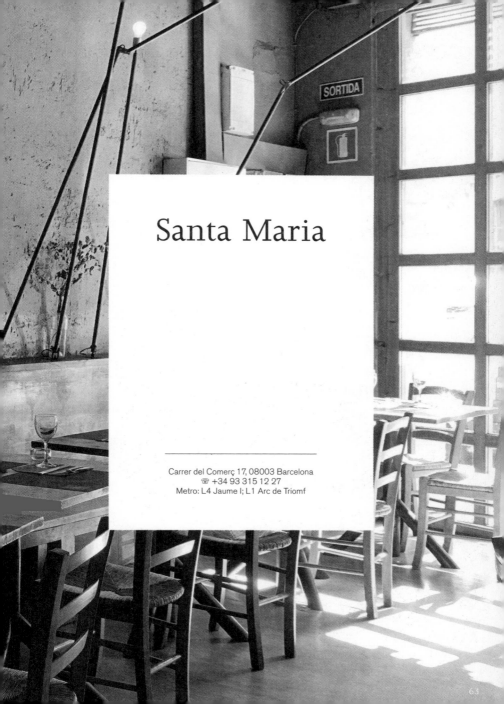

Santa Maria

Carrer del Comerç 17, 08003 Barcelona
☎ +34 93 315 12 27
Metro: L4 Jaume I; L1 Arc de Triomf

Bar Gimlet

Carrer del Rec 24, 08001 Barcelona
☎ +34 93 310 10 27
Metro: L4 Jaume I

La Paradeta

Carrer Comercial 7, 08003 Barcelona
☏ +34 93 268 19 39
www.laparadeta.com
Metro: L4 Barceloneta/Jaume I

El Xampanyet

Carrer de Montcada 22, 08003 Barcelona
☎ +34 93 319 70 03
Metro: L4 Jaume I

Salero

Carrer del Rec 60, 08003 Barcelona
☎ +34 93 319 80 22
Metro: L4 Barceloneta

La Vinya del Senyor

Plaça de Santa Maria 5, 08003 Barcelona
☎ +34 93 310 33 79
Metro: L4 Jaume I

Passadís del Pep

Pla de Palau 2, 08003 Barcelona
☎ +34 93 310 10 21
www.passadis.com
Metro: L4 Barceloneta

Granja La Pallaresa

Carrer de Petritxol 11
08001 Barcelona
☎ +34 93 302 20 36

pp. 32/33

Traditional Milk Bar
Interior: Like when it opened in 1947

Open: Daily 9am–1pm and 4–9pm | **X-Factor:** The "suizo" |
Prices: Suizo as of 2.05 €.
A "suizo", a hot chocolate-pudding-like drink with lots of cream, and a deep-fried "churro" are simply part and parcel of any visit to Barcelona.

Öffnungszeiten: Täglich 9–13 und 16–21 Uhr | **X-Faktor:**
Der „suizo" | **Preise:** Suizo ab 2,05 €.
Ein „suizo", ein heißes schokoladenpuddingartiges Getränk mit ganz viel Sahne, und ein in Fett gebackener „churro" gehören zu jedem Barcelona-Besuch.

Horaires d'ouverture : Tous les jours 9h–13h et 16h–21h |
Le « petit plus » : Le « suizo » | **Prix :** Suizo à partir de 2,05 € | A déguster impérativement quand on visite Barcelone : le « suizo », une boisson chaude chocolatée avec beaucoup de crème, et le « churro », une sorte de beignet.

Caelum

Carrer de la Palla 8
08002 Barcelona
☎ +34 93 302 69 93

pp. 38/39

Tea Room & Pastry Shop
Atmosphere: On the site of medieval Jewish baths

Open: Daily 10.30am–2pm and 5–9pm | **X-Factor:** Special-
ities from 38 Spanish monasteries | **Prices:** Tea from 2.50 €.
Tea is served with specialities from Spanish monasteries, such as fine marzipan cakes.

Öffnungszeiten: Täglich 10.30–14 und 17–21 Uhr |
X-Faktor: Die Spezialitäten aus 38 spanischen Klöstern |
Preise: Tee ab 2,50 €.
Zum Tee gibt es Spezialitäten aus spanischen Klöstern – wie feinen Marzipankuchen.

Horaires d'ouverture : Tous les jours 10h30–14h et 17h–21h | **Le « petit plus » :** Les spécialités provenant de 38 monastères espagnols | **Prix :** Thé à partir de 2,50 €.
Avec le thé vous dégusterez les spécialités des monastères espagnols, comme le délicieux gâteau au massepain.

Cafè d'Estiu

Plaça de Sant Iu 5–6
08002 Barcelona
☎ +34 93 268 25 98
www.museumares.bcn.es
www.textilcafe.com

pp. 42/43

Romantic Summer Café
Atmosphere: Under orange trees

Open: 1 April to 30 September, daily 10am–10pm |
X-Factor: The nearby Museu Frederic Marès | **Prices:**
Coffee from 1.20 €.
This idyllic café is like an oasis, hidden on the patio of the old palace of the Counts of Barcelona.

Öffnungszeiten: 1. April bis 30. September, täglich 10–
22 Uhr | **X-Faktor:** Das Museu Frederic Marès nebenan |
Preise: Kaffee ab 1,20 €.
Das idyllische Café gleicht einer Oase und versteckt sich im Patio des alten Palastes der Grafen von Barcelona.

Horaires d'ouverture : 1er avril au 30 septembre, tous les jours 10h–22h | **Le « petit plus » :** Le Museu Frederic Marès situé à côté | **Prix :** Café à partir de 1,20 €.
Véritable oasis de paix, ce café idyllique est niché dans le patio du vieux palais des comtes de Barcelone.

La Torna

Mercat de Santa Caterina
Avinguda de Francesc Cambó 16
08003 Barcelona
☎ +34 93 319 58 21

pp. 46/47

Atmospheric Market Bar
Atmosphere: In the Santa Caterina covered market

Open: Daily 8am–11pm | **X-Factor:** You feel like a local |
Prices: Meals from 5–15 €.
Everything about this unpretentious bar is good, from the fresh tapas to the strong coffee.

Öffnungszeiten: Täglich 8–23 Uhr | **X-Faktor:** Man fühlt sich wie ein Einheimischer | **Preise:** Gerichte 5–15 €.
Von den frischen Tapas bis zum kräftigen Kaffee: An dieser unprätentiösen Bar ist alles gut!

Horaires d'ouverture : Tous les jours 8h–23h | **Le « petit plus » :** On a l'impression d'être un autochtone | **Prix :** Plats 5–15 €.
Des tapas toutes fraîches au café corsé – dans ce café sans prétention tout est délicieux !

Cuines Santa Caterina

Mercat de Santa Caterina
Avinguda de Francesc Cambó 20
08003 Barcelona
☎ +34 93 268 99 18
www.grupotragaluz.com

pp. 48/49

Chic Market Restaurant
Design: Enric Miralles

Open: Daily 1–4pm and 8pm–midnight | **X-Factor:** The place mat is also the menu | **Prices:** Meals from 4–20 €.
This excellent restaurant is well integrated into the market, which was designed as a homage to Gaudí.

Öffnungszeiten: Täglich 13–16 und 20–24 Uhr | **X-Faktor:** Das Tischset dient zugleich als Speisekarte | **Preise:** Gerichte 4–20 €.
Das exzellente Lokal ist sehr gelungen in die neuen Markthallen integriert, die als Hommage an Gaudí gestaltet wurden.

Horaires d'ouverture : Tous les jours 13h–16h et 20h– 24h | **Le « petit plus » :** Le set de table sert aussi de carte | **Prix :** Plats 4–20 €.
Excellent restaurant, très bien intégré aux nouvelles halles dont la forme rend hommage à Gaudí.

Restaurant Borràs l'Econòmic

Plaça de Sant Agustí Vell 13
08003 Barcelona
☎ +34 93 319 64 94

pp. 58/59

Authentic Lunch Restaurant
Interior: Unchanged since 1932

Open: Daily 1–4pm | **X-Factor:** Menu changes daily | **Prices:** Lunch with wine from 8 €.
The interior is a successful mix of mirrors, colourful azulejos and old oil-paintings – good and affordable traditional Catalan food is served at lunch-time.

Öffnungszeiten: Täglich 13–16 Uhr | **X-Faktor:** Die Speisekarte wechselt täglich | **Preise:** Lunch mit Wein ab 8 €.
Das Interieur mischt gekonnt Spiegel, bunte Azulejos und alte Ölbilder – hier bekommt man mittags gute und preiswerte katalanische Hausmannskost.

Horaires d'ouverture : Tous les jours 13h–16h | **Le « petit plus » :** La carte change quotidiennement | **Prix :** Déjeuner, vin compris, à partir de 8 € | Intérieur mariant les miroirs, les azulejos de couleur et les anciens tableaux à l'huile. Cuisine catalane traditionnelle, goûteuse et pas chère, le midi.

Mundial Bar

Plaça de Sant Agustí Vell 1
08003 Barcelona
☎ +34 93 319 90 56

pp. 54/55

Simple Tapas Bar
Interior: Unpretentious 1920s

Open: Tu 9pm–11pm, We–Su 1pm–4pm, We–Fr 9pm–11pm, Sa 9pm–11.30pm | **X-Factor:** Smoking still permitted | **Prices:** Simple tapas from 4 €.
This bar has been one of the neighbourhood's most popular places since 1925 – authentic and full of atmosphere.

Öffnungszeiten: Di 21–23, Mi–So 13–16, Mi–Fr 21–23, Sa 21–23.30 Uhr | **X-Faktor:** Hier herrscht noch kein Rauchverbot | **Preise:** Einfache Tapas ab 4 €.
Seit 1925 gehört diese Bar zu den Lieblingsplätzen der Nachbarschaft – sie ist authentisch und atmosphärisch.

Horaires d'ouverture : Mar 21h–23h, Mer–Dim 13h–16h, Mer–Ven 21h–23h, Sam 21h–23h30 | **Le « petit plus » :** Pas encore d'interdiction de fumer | **Prix :** Tapas simples à partir de 4 € | Authentique et couleur locale, ce bar est l'un des lieux les plus appréciés du quartier depuis 1925.

Santa Maria

Carrer del Comerç 17
08003 Barcelona
☎ +34 93 315 12 27

pp. 62/63

Avant-garde Tapas Restaurant
Interior: Does not distract from the food

Open: Tu–Sa 1.30–3.30pm and 8.30pm–midnight | **X-Factor:** No endless queues like in elBulli | **Prices:** degustation menu 30 €.
Paco Guzmán trained under Ferran Adrià – creative people in this city quarter appreciate his unusual tapas variations.

Öffnungszeiten: Di–Sa 13.30–15.30 und 20.30–24 Uhr | **X-Faktor:** Hier gibt es keine Endlos-Wartezeiten wie im elBulli | **Preise:** Degustations-Menü 30 €.
Paco Guzmán lernte bei Ferran Adrià – die Kreativen des Viertels schätzen seine ungewöhnlichen Tapas-Kreationen.

Horaires d'ouverture : Mar–Sam 13h30–15h30 et 20h30–24h | **Le « petit plus » :** Pas de longue file d'attente comme chez elBulli | **Prix :** Menu dégustation 30 €.
Paco Guzmán a eu Ferran Adrià pour maître. Les créatifs du quartier apprécient l'originalité de ses tapas.

Bar Gimlet

Carrer del Rec 24
08001 Barcelona
☎ +34 93 310 10 27

pp. 66/67

La Paradeta

Carrer Comercial 7
08003 Barcelona
☎ +34 93 268 19 39
www.laparadeta.com

pp. 70/71

Sophisticated Cocktail Bar
Interior: Intimate

Open: Mo–Sa 8pm–3am | **X-Factor:** The Whiskey Sour |
Prices: Cocktails as of 5 €.
This bar got its name from detective Philip Marlowe's favourite drink; and not only the gimlet is perfectly mixed.

Öffnungszeiten: Mo–Sa 20–3 Uhr | **X-Faktor:** Der Whiskey Sour | **Preise:** Cocktails ab 5 €.
Diese Cocktail-Bar erhielt ihren Namen vom Lieblingsdrink des Detektivs Philip Marlowe; nicht nur der Gimlet ist perfekt gemixt.

Horaires d'ouverture : Lun–Sam 20h–3h | **Le « petit plus » :** Le Whiskey Sour | **Prix :** Cocktails à partir de 5 €.
Ce bar tient son nom de la boisson préférée du détective Philip Marlowe, mais le Gimlet n'est pas le seul cocktail parfaitement mixé.

Fish & Seafood Eatery
Atmosphere: Self-service

Open: Tu–Fr 8am–11.30pm; Sa 1–4pm and 8pm–midnight; Su 1–4pm | **X-Factor:** Good selection of wines for the fish | **Prices:** 1 kilo fish from 13 € | You select your fish at the market stand ("paradeta") and it is served across the counter freshly prepared – "a la plancha" (grilled) or simply fried.

Öffnungszeiten: Di–Fr 8–23.30, Sa 13–16 und 20–24, So 13–16 Uhr | **X-Faktor:** Die gute Weinauswahl zum Fisch | **Preise:** 1 Kilo Fisch ab 13 € | Am Marktstand („paradeta") wählt man seinen Fisch aus und bekommt ihn dann frisch zubereitet – „a la plancha" (gegrillt) oder gebraten über die Theke gereicht.

Horaires d'ouverture : Mar–Ven 8h–23h30, Sam 13h–16h et 20h–24h, Dim 13h–16h | **Le « petit plus » :** Bon choix de vins | **Prix :** 1 kilo de poisson à partir de 13 € | Le poisson est choisi à l'étal (« paradeta ») puis préparé « a la plancha » (grillé) ou cuit à la poêle. Il est servi au comptoir.

El Xampanyet

Carrer de Montcada 22
08003 Barcelona
☎ +34 93 319 70 03

pp. 74/75

Salero

Carrer del Rec 60
08003 Barcelona
☎ +34 93 319 80 22

pp. 80/81

Cava & Tapas Bar
Interior: Almost totally original 1929

Open: Tu–Sa midday–4pm and 7–11.30pm | **X-Factor:** The home-made tapas | **Prices:** Cava from 1.20 €.
The delicious, well-cooled "cava" (Spanish champagne) ensures that this original family-run bar is always full.

Öffnungszeiten: Di–Sa 12–16 und 19–23.30 Uhr | **X-Faktor:** Die hausgemachten Tapas | **Preise:** Cava ab 1,20 € | Der köstliche und gut gekühlte „cava" (spanischer Champagner) sorgt dafür, dass diese urige, familiengeführte Bar immer voll ist.

Horaires d'ouverture : Mar–Sam 12h–16h et 19h–23h30 | **Le « petit plus » :** Les tapas maison | **Prix :** Cava à partir de 1,20 € | On y sert un délicieux « cava » bien frais (Champagne espagnol), ce qui explique pourquoi ce bar pittoresque et familial est toujours bondé.

Fusion Kitchen
Design: Pilar Líbano

Open: Mo–We 1.30–4pm and 9pm–midnight; Th/Fr 1–4pm and 9pm–1am; Sa 9pm–1am | **X-Factor:** The successful mix of furniture | **Prices:** Lunch c. 15 €, dinner c. 30 €.
Once a salt store ("salero"), today a stylish restaurant decorated in white, with European-Japanese fusion food.

Öffnungszeiten: Mo–Mi 13.30–16 und 21–24, Do/Fr 13–16 und 21–1, Sa 21–1 Uhr | **X-Faktor:** Der gekonnte Möbel-Mix | **Preise:** Lunch um 15 €, Dinner um 30 €.
Einst ein Salzlager („salero"), heute ein stylisches Lokal in Weiß gestaltet und mit europäisch-japanischer Fusion Cuisine.

Horaires d'ouverture : Lun–Mer 13h30–16h et 21h–24h, Jeu/Ven 13h–16h et 21h–1h, Sam 21h–1h | **Le « petit plus » :** Le savant méli-mélo de meubles | **Prix :** Déjeuner env. 15 €, dîner env. 30 € | Ancien entrepôt de sel cet établissement tendance propose une Cuisine Fusion sino-européenne.

La Vinya del Senyor

Plaça de Santa Maria 5
08003 Barcelona
☎ +34 93 310 33 79

pp. 86/87

Passadís del Pep

Pla de Palau 2
08003 Barcelona
☎ +34 93 310 10 21
www.passadis.com

pp. 90/91

Wine & Tapas Bar
Interior: Shelves with more than 250 different wines

Open: Tu–Su midday–1pm | **X-Factor:** Seats outside with a view of Santa Maria del Mar | **Prices:** Wine from 1.75 €.
Good selection of wines from all over the world, tapas from Catalunya – the "bacallà amb tomàquet" is to be recommended.

Öffnungszeiten: Di–So 12–1 Uhr | **X-Faktor:** Die Außenplätze mit Blick auf Santa Maria del Mar | **Preise:** Wein ab 1,75 €.
Die gut sortierten Weine stammen aus aller Welt, die Tapas aus Katalonien – besonders gut ist „bacallà amb tomàquet".

Horaires d'ouverture : Mar–Dim 12h–1h | **Le « petit plus »** : Les places en terrasse avec vue sur Santa Maria del Mar | **Prix** : Vin à partir de 1,75 € | Très bon choix de vins du monde entier et tapas de Catalogne. A goûter absolument : la « bacallà amb tomàquet ».

Fine Dining Fish Restaurant
Interior: 19th century vault

Open: Mo 9–1.30pm; Tu–Sa 1.30–3.30 and 9–11.30pm | **X-Factor:** No menu; you take what the chef recommends | **Prices:** Menu c. 80 €.
Not easy to find, but worth the search – one of the best fish restaurants in town.

Öffnungszeiten: Mo 21–23.30, Di–Sa 13.30–15.30 und 21–23.30 Uhr | **X-Faktor:** Es gibt keine Karte, man folgt dem Rat des Chefs | **Preise:** Menü um 80 €.
Das Lokal ist nicht leicht zu finden, belohnt die Suche aber – eines der besten Fischrestaurants der Stadt.

Horaires d'ouverture : Lun 21h–23h30, Mar–Sam 13h30–15h30 et 21h–23h30 | **Le « petit plus »** : Pas de carte, on suit les recommandations du chef | **Prix** : Menu env. 80 €.
Pas facile à trouver, mais l'un des meilleurs restaurants de poisson de la ville.

La Barceloneta

Cervecería
El Vaso de Oro

Carrer de Balboa 6, 08003 Barcelona
☎ +34 93 319 30 98
Metro: L4 Barceloneta

Bestial

Carrer de Ramon Trias Fargas 2–4, 08005 Barcelona
☎ +34 93 224 04 07
www.bestialdeltragaluz.com
Metro: L4 Ciutadella Vila Olímpica

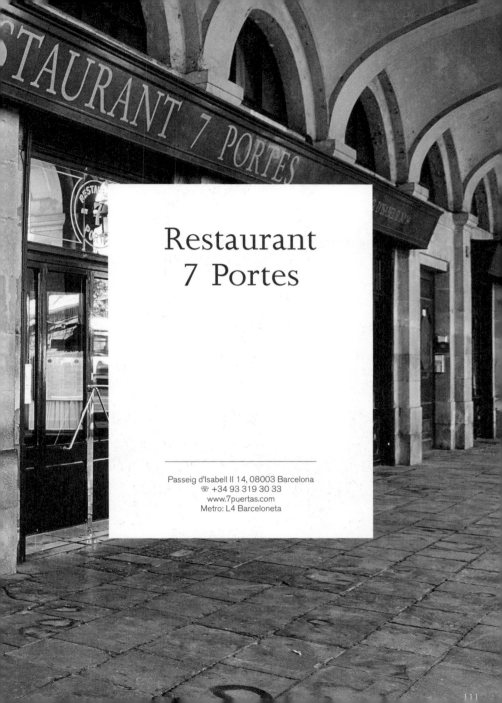

Restaurant 7 Portes

Passeig d'Isabell II 14, 08003 Barcelona
☎ +34 93 319 30 33
www.7puertas.com
Metro: L4 Barceloneta

Torre
d'Alta Mar

Passeig de Joan de Borbó 88, 08039 Barcelona
☎ +34 93 221 00 07
www.torredealtamar.com
Metro: L4 Barceloneta

Cervecería El Vaso de Oro

Carrer de Balboa 6
08003 Barcelona
☎ +34 93 319 30 98

pp. 100/101

Rustic Beer & Tapas Bar
Interior: Maritime with mahogany

Open: Daily 8am–midnight | **X-Factor:** Large beer selection |
Prices: Tapas from 4–15 €.
The locals meet at this original bar in the former fishermen's quarter for a glass of something to drink and some excellent tapas.

Öffnungszeiten: Täglich 8–24 Uhr | **X-Faktor:** Die große Bier-Auswahl | **Preise:** Tapas 4–15 €.
In dieser urigen Bar im einstigen Fischerviertel treffen sich die Einheimischen am Tresen auf ein Glas und essen exzellente Tapas.

Horaires d'ouverture : Tous les jours 8h–24h | **Le « petit plus » :** Le grand choix de bières | **Prix :** Tapas 4–15 €.
Dans ce bar très couleur locale, situé dans l'ancien quartier des pêcheurs, les autochtones se rencontrent au comptoir autour d'un verre et d'excellentes tapas.

Bestial

Carrer de Ramon Trias
Fargas 2–4
08005 Barcelona
☎ +34 93 224 04 07
www.bestialdeltragaluz.com

pp. 104/105

Minimalist Mediterranean Restaurant
Design: Tarruella & Lopez

Open: Mo–Fr 1–3.45pm and 8–11.30pm (Fr till 0.30 am); Sa 1pm–4.30 and 8pm–0.30am; Su 1pm–4.30 and 8–11.30pm | **X-Factor:** The 350-square-metre terrace with a view of the sea | **Prices:** Meals from 8–20 €.
Fine Italian food served in a minimalist atmosphere.

Öffnungszeiten: Mo–Fr 13–15.45 und 20–23.30 (Fr bis 0.30), Sa 13–16.30 und 20–0.30, So 13–16.30 und 20–23.30 Uhr | **X-Faktor:** Die 350-qm-Terrasse mit Blick aufs Meer | **Preise:** Gerichte 8–20 € | In minimalistischem Ambiente wird feine italienische Küche serviert.

Horaires d'ouverture : Lun–Ven 13h–15h45 et 20h–23h30 (Ven jusqu'à 0h30), Sam 13h–16h30 et 20h–0h30, Dim 13h–16h30 et 20h–23h30 | **Le « petit plus » :** La terrasse de 350m² avec vue sur la mer | **Prix :** Plats 8–20 €.
Cuisine italienne raffinée servie dans un décor minimaliste.

Restaurant 7 Portes

Passeig d'Isabell II 14
08003 Barcelona
☎ +34 93 319 30 33
www.7puertas.com

pp. 110/111

Legendary Paella Restaurant
Interior: In the "Pòrtics d'en Xifré", a national monument

Open: Daily 1pm–1am | **X-Factor:** Plaques to famous guests like Che Guevara and Orson Welles | **Prices:** Paella from 13 €.
In the city's oldest restaurant (since 1836) old-style waiters serve paella variations and sea-food.

Öffnungszeiten: Täglich 13–1 Uhr | **X-Faktor:** Plaketten erinnern an berühmte Gäste wie Che Guevara und Orson Welles | **Preise:** Paella ab 13 €.
Im ältesten Restaurant der Stadt (seit 1836) servieren Kellner der alten Schule Paella-Variationen und Meeresfrüchte.

Horaires d'ouverture : Tous les jours 13h–1h | **Le « petit plus » :** Clients célèbres comme Che Guevara et Orson Welles | **Prix :** Paella à partir de 13 € | Dans le plus ancien restaurant de la ville (depuis 1836), des serveurs de la vieille école vous apportent des variations de paella et des fruits de mer.

Torre d'Alta Mar

Passeig de Joan de Borbó 88
08039 Barcelona
☎ +34 93 221 00 07
www.torredealtamar.com

pp. 114/115

Mediterranean Panorama Restaurant
Interior: Up in the Torre de Sant Sebastià (built for Expo 1929)

Open: Daily 1pm–3.30 and 7–11.30pm | **X-Factor:** "Mar i Muntanya" (lobster & guinea fowl) | **Prices:** Menu c. 80 €.
At a height of 75 metres, a breathtaking 360-degree panorama and fresh sea-food.

Öffnungszeiten: Täglich 13–15.30 und 19–23.30 Uhr | **X-Faktor:** "Mar i Muntanya" (Hummer & Perlhuhn) | **Preise:** Menü um 80 €.
In 75 Metern Höhe warten ein atemberaubendes 360-Grad-Panorama und frische Meeresfrüchte.

Horaires d'ouverture : Tous les jours 13h–15h30 et 19h–23h30 | **Le « petit plus » :** « Mar i Muntanya » (langouste & pintade) | **Prix :** Menu env. 80 € | Un panorama époustouflant de 360° et des fruits de mer d'une grande fraîcheur vous attendent à 75 mètres de hauteur.

L'Eixample
Gràcia
Tibidabo

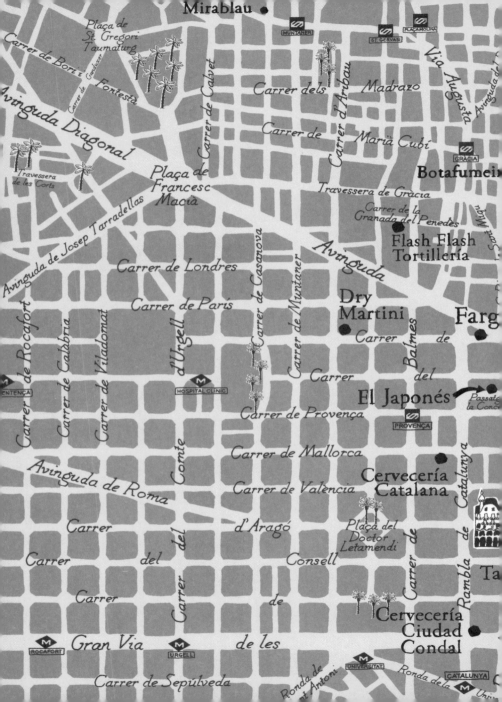

Cervecería
Ciudad Condal

Rambla de Catalunya 18, 08007 Barcelona
☎ +34 93 318 19 97
Metro: L2, L3, L4 Passeig de Gràcia

Noti

Carrer de Roger de Llúria 35–37, 08009 Barcelona
☎ +34 93 342 66 73
www.noti-universal.com
Metro: L2, L3, L4 Passeig de Gràcia

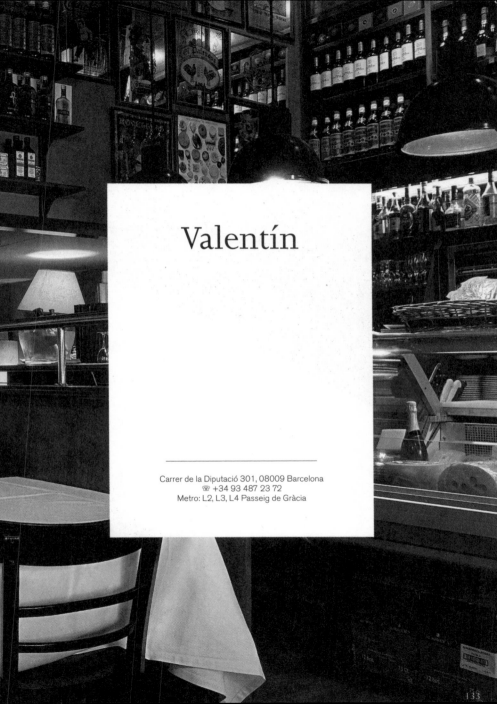

Valentín

Carrer de la Diputació 301, 08009 Barcelona
☎ +34 93 487 23 72
Metro: L2, L3, L4 Passeig de Gràcia

TapaÇ24

Carrer de la Diputació 269, 08007 Barcelona
☎ +34 93 488 09 77
www.carlesabellan.com
Metro: L2, L3, L4 Passeig de Gràcia

Cervecería
Catalana

Carrer de Mallorca 236, 08007 Barcelona
☎ +34 93 216 03 68
Metro: L2, L3, L4 Passeig de Gràcia

El Japonés

Passatge de la Concepció 2, 08008 Barcelona
☏ +34 93 487 25 92
www.eljaponesdeltragaluz.com
Metro: L3, L5 Diagonal

Bar Mut

Carrer de Pau Claris 192, 08037 Barcelona
☏ +34 93 217 43 38
Metro: L3, L5 Diagonal

Farga

Avinguda Diagonal 391, 08008 Barcelona
☎ +34 93 416 01 12
www.fargabarcelona.com
Metro: L3, L5 Diagonal

Dry Martini

Carrer d'Aribau 162–166, 08036 Barcelona
☎ +34 93 217 50 72
www.drymartinibcn.com
Metro: L3, L5 Diagonal

Flash Flash
Tortillería

Carrer de la Granada del Penedès 25, 08006 Barcelona
☎ +34 93 237 09 90
www.flashflashtortilleria.com
Metro: L3, L5 Diagonal

Botafumeiro

Carrer Gran de Gràcia 81, 08012 Barcelona
☏ +34 93 218 42 30
www.botafumeiro.es
Metro: L3 Fontana

Mirablau

Plaça del Doctor Andreu, 08035 Barcelona
☎ +34 93 418 58 79
Metro: L7 Avinguda Tibidabo

Cervecería Ciudad Condal

Rambla de Catalunya 18
08007 Barcelona
☎ +34 93 318 19 97

pp. 124/125

Popular Tapas Restaurant
Interior: Great window seats onto the Rambla

Open: Mo–Fr 7am–1.30pm; Sa/Su 9am–1.20am |
X-Factor: The "montaditos" (canapés) | **Prices:** tapas from
4–12 €.
Huge selection of tapas, friendly atmosphere: this restaurant
is always a good place to stop at!

Öffnungszeiten: Mo–Fr 7–1.30, Sa/So 9–1.30 Uhr |
X-Faktor: Die „montaditos" (belegte Brote) | **Preise:** Tapas
4–12 €.
Die Auswahl an Tapas ist riesengroß, die Atmosphäre freund-
lich: Dieses Lokal ist immer ein guter Zwischenstopp!

Horaires d'ouverture : Lun–Ven 7h–1h30, Sam/Dim
9h–1h30 | **Le « petit plus » :** Les « montaditos » (canapés) |
Prix : Tapas 4–12 €.
Enorme choix de tapas, ambiance amicale, il fait toujours bon
s'y arrêter !

Noti

Carrer de Roger
de Llúria 35–37
08009 Barcelona
☎ +34 93 342 66 73
www.noti-universal.com

pp. 128/129

Glamorous Restaurant & Bar
Design: Francesc Pons

Open: Mo–Fr 1.30pm–4 and 8.30pm–midnight; Sa/So
8.30pm–midnight | **X-Factor:** To see and be seen | **Prices:**
lunch menu 19 €; a la carte from 15–32 €.
The interior colours are inspired by the corrida, the menu by
European modernism.

Öffnungszeiten: Mo–Fr 13.30–16 und 20.30–24, Sa/So
20.30–24 Uhr | **X-Faktor:** Sehen und gesehen werden |
Preise: Lunch-Menü 19 €, Gerichte 15–32 €.
Das Interieur ist in den Farben vom Stierkampf inspiriert, das
Menü von der europäischen Moderne.

Horaires d'ouverture : Lun–Ven 13h30–16h et 20h30–
24h, Sam/Dim 20h30–24h | **Le « petit plus » :** Voir et être
vu | **Prix :** Menu de midi 19 €, Plats 15–32 € | L'intérieur
s'inspire des couleurs de la corrida, le menu des tendances
modernes européennes.

Valentín

Carrer de la Diputació 301
08009 Barcelona
☎ +34 93 487 23 72

pp. 132/133

Catalan Restaurant
Interior: On two well-used levels

Open: Daily 1pm–4.30 and 8.30–11.30pm | **X-Factor:** The
"Xarcutería" next door | **Prices:** Lunch menu c. 15 €.
At lunch-time, guests can select from two freshly-prepared
fish or meat dishes.

Öffnungszeiten: Täglich 13–16.30 und 20.30–23.30 Uhr |
X-Faktor: Die angeschlossene „Xarcutería" | **Preise:** Lunch-
Menü um 15 €.
Mittags wählen die Berufstätigen des Viertels hier aus zwei
frisch zubereiteten Menüs mit Fisch oder Fleisch.

Horaires d'ouverture : Tous les jours 13h–16h30 et
20h30–23h30 | **Le « petit plus » :** La « Xarcutería » adja-
cente | **Prix :** Menu de midi env. 15 € | Ceux qui font leur
pause-midi dans le quartier ont le choix entre un menu avec
de la viande et un autre avec du poisson.

TapaÇ24

Carrer de la Diputació 269
08007 Barcelona
☎ +34 93 488 09 77
www.carlesabellan.com

pp. 136/137

Classic Tapas Bar
Interior: Simple, basement

Open: Mo–Sa 8am–midnight | **X-Factor:** The "BikiniÇ24"
tapas with Jamón Ibérico, mozzarella and truffles | **Prices:**
Tapas from 1.50–14 €.
A bar with an uncomplicated atmosphere, super-fresh tapas
and prompt service.

Öffnungszeiten: Mo–Sa 8–24 Uhr | **X-Faktor:** Die Tapas
„BikiniÇ24" mit Jamón Ibérico, Mozzarella und Trüffel |
Preise: Tapas 1,50–14 €.
Eine Bar mit unkompliziertem Ambiente, superfrischen Tapas
und schnellem Service.

Horaires d'ouverture : Lun–Sam 8h–24h | **Le « petit
plus » :** Les tapas « BikiniÇ24 » au Jamón Ibérico, mozzarelle
et truffe | **Prix :** Tapas 1,50–14 €.
Un bar où on ne fait pas de chichis et qui offre des tapas
super fraîches et un service rapide.

Cervecería Catalana

Carrer de Mallorca 236
08007 Barcelona
☎ +34 93 216.03 68

pp. 140/141

El Japonés

Passatge de la Concepció 2
08008 Barcelona
☎ +34 93 487 25 92
www.eljaponesdeltragaluz.com

pp. 144/145

Traditional Tapas Bar
Interior: Two long bars and cosy seating

Open: Daily 1pm–1am | **X-Factor:** Meeting place for the locals | **Prices:** Tapas from 1.50 €.
Barcelona's oldest tapas bar, where everything is just right: a huge choice of tapas, top quality, and the cava and beer are well cooled.

Öffnungszeiten: Täglich 13–1 Uhr | **X-Faktor:** Hier trifft man viele Einheimische | **Preise:** Tapas ab 1,50 €.
In Barcelonas ältester Tapas-Bar stimmt alles: Die Auswahl an Tapas ist riesig, die Qualität ausgezeichnet und der Cava und das Bier gut gekühlt.

Horaires d'ouverture : Tous les jours 13h–1h | **Le « petit plus » :** On rencontre ici beaucoup d'autochtones | **Prix :** Tapas à partir de 1,50 € | Dans ce plus vieux bar à tapas de Barcelone, tout est pour le mieux : immense choix de tapas, excellente qualité, bière et cava bien frais.

Minimalist Japanese Restaurant
Design: Tarruella & Lopez

Open: Lunch daily 1.30pm–4pm; dinner Su–We 8.30pm–midnight; Th 8pm–0.30am; Fr/Sa 8pm–1am | **Prices:** Located in a quiet pedestrian passage-way | **Prices:** Meals from 18–28 € | The excellent kushiyaki and sushi attract a mixed young clientele.

Öffnungszeiten: Lunch täglich 13.30–16 Uhr, Dinner So–Mi 20.30–24, Do 20–0.30, Fr/Sa 20–1 Uhr | **X-Faktor:** Die Lage in einer autofreien Passage | **Preise:** Gerichte 18–28 € | Die ausgezeichneten Kushiyaki und Sushi ziehen ein junges, gemischtes Publikum an.

Horaires d'ouverture : Déjeuner tous les jours 13h30–16h, dîner Dim–Mer 20h30–24h, Jeu 20h–0h.30, Ven/Sam 20h–1h | **Le « petit plus » :** Situé dans une rue piétonne | **Prix :** Plats 18–28 € | Les excellents kushiyaki et sushi attirent un public jeune et hétéroclite.

Bar Mut

Carrer de Pau Claris 192
08037 Barcelona
☎ +34 93 217 43 38

pp. 148/149

Farga

Avinguda Diagonal 391
08008 Barcelona
☎ +34 93 416.01 12
www.fargabarcelona.com

pp. 152/153

Tapas & Wine Bar
Interior: Classical

Open: Mo–Fr 8am–midnight; Sa/Su midday–midnight | **X-Factor:** Obliging service | **Prices:** Tapas from 3 €.
A pleasant bar with the flair of an up-market bodega. The many regulars share the owner's passion for good wines.

Öffnungszeiten: Mo–Fr 8–24, Sa/So 12–24 Uhr | **X-Faktor:** Der zuvorkommende Service | **Preise:** Tapas ab 3 € | Eine sympathische Bar im Stil einer gehobenen Bodega. Die vielen Stammgäste teilen die Leidenschaft des Besitzers für guten Wein.

Horaires d'ouverture : Lun–Ven 8h–24h, Sam/Dim 12h–24h | **Le « petit plus » :** Les serveurs attentifs | **Prix :** Tapas à partir de 3 € | Un bar sympathique dans le style d'une bodega très classe. Les nombreux habitués partagent leur amour du bon vin avec le propriétaire.

Elegant Restaurant, Tearoom & Pastry Shop
Interior: 1960s style

Open: Mo–Fr 8am–midnight; Sa 9am–midnight; Su 9am–11pm | **X-Factor:** The seats at the long counter | **Prices:** Menu c. 30 €.
A classic – for enjoyable fresh salads and sandwiches, delicious cakes and excellent service.

Öffnungszeiten: Mo–Fr 8–24, Sa 9–24, So 9–23 Uhr | **X-Faktor:** Die Plätze an der langen Theke | **Preise:** Menü um 30 €.
Ein Klassiker – hier genießt man frische Salate und Sandwiches, köstliche Kuchen und einen exzellenten Service.

Horaires d'ouverture : Lun–Ven 8h–24h, Sam 9h–24h, Dim 9h–23h | **Le « petit plus » :** Les places au long comptoir | **Prix :** Menu env. 30 €.
Un classique de la gastronomie : salades et sandwiches frais, gâteaux succulents et service excellent.

Dry Martini

Carrer d'Aribau 162–166
08036 Barcelona
☎ +34 93 217 50 72
www.drymartinibcn.com

pp. 156/157

Famous Cocktail Bar
Interior: Almost a cocktail-museum

Open: Su–Th 1pm–2.30am; Fr/Sa 1pm–3am | **X-Factor:** A "must" in Barcelona | **Prices:** Dry Martinis from 7 €.
For 007's favourite drink they have more than 80 types of gin on their shelves.

Öffnungszeiten: So–Do 13–2.30, Fr/Sa 13–3 Uhr | **X-Faktor:** Ein „must" in Barcelona | **Preise:** Dry Martini ab 7 €.
Für den Lieblingsdrink von 007 stehen mehr als 80 Sorten Gin in den Regalen.

Horaires d'ouverture : Dim–Jeu 13h–2h30, Ven/Sam 13h–3h | **Le « petit plus » :** Un « must » à Barcelone | **Prix :** Martini dry à partir de 7 €.
Plus de 80 variétés de gin se trouvent sur les étagères pour préparer la boisson favorite de 007.

Flash Flash Tortillería

Carrer de la Granada del Penedès 25
08006 Barcelona
☎ +34 93 237 09 90
www.flashflashtortilleria.com

pp. 160/161

Stylish Tortillería
Design: The black silhouettes on the wall are of model Karin Leiz

Open: Daily 1pm–1.30am | **X-Factor:** More than 70 different tortillas | **Prices:** From 8 €.
A journey back in time to the 70s: opened in 1970, it is still very stylish.

Öffnungszeiten: Täglich 13–1.30 Uhr | **X-Faktor:** Mehr als 70 Tortilla-Variationen | **Preise:** Ab 8 €.
Eine Zeitreise in die Siebziger: Das Lokal wurde 1970 eröffnet und ist immer noch superstylisch.

Horaires d'ouverture : Tous les jours 13h–1h30 | **Le « petit plus » :** Plus de 70 variétés de tortillas | **Prix :** À partir de 8 € |
Un voyage dans le temps. L'établissement a ouvert ses portes en 1970 et est toujours très stylish.

Botafumeiro

Carrer Gran de Gràcia 81
08012 Barcelona
☎ +34 93 218 42 30
www.botafumeiro.es

pp. 166/167

Classic Fish Restaurant
Interior: The best place to sit is "en la barra", at the bar

Open: Mo–Su 1pm–1am | **X-Factor:** The old-style menus for ladies, with no prices | **Prices:** Meals from 20–40 €.
The fish and sea-food recipes for their elegant late dinners are from northern Spain.

Öffnungszeiten: Mo–So 13–1 Uhr | **X-Faktor:** Die alt-modischen Menükarten ohne Preise für Damen | **Preise:** Gerichte 20–40 €.
Beim eleganten späten Dinner werden hier Fisch und Meeres-früchte nach nordspanischen Rezepten serviert.

Horaires d'ouverture : Lun–Dim 13h–1h | **Le « petit plus » :** La carte pour dames, sans les prix | **Prix :** Plats 20–40 € | Préparés selon des recettes du nord de l'Espagne, le poisson et les fruits de mer sont servis tard le soir au cours de dîners élégants.

Mirablau

Plaça del Doctor Andreu
08035 Barcelona
☎ +34 93 418 58 79

pp. 170/171

Tibidabo Panorama Bar
Interior: The window seats are much coveted

Open: Daily 11am–5am | **X-Factor:** The bar is a disco at night | **Prices:** Drinks from 2.40–8 €.
The mixed clientele can enjoy a breathtaking view of Barcelona's sea of lights.

Öffnungszeiten: Täglich 11–5 Uhr | **X-Faktor:** Nachts wird die Bar zur Disco | **Preise:** Getränke 2,40–8 €.
Ein gemischtes Publikum genießt eine atemberaubende Aussicht auf das Häuser- und Lichtermeer von Barcelona.

Horaires d'ouverture : Tous les jours 11h-5h | **Le « petit plus » :** La nuit le bar se transforme en discothèque | **Prix :** Boissons 2,40–8 €.
Le public hétéroclite jouit d'une vue splendide sur les maisons et les illuminations de Barcelone.

Poble Sec
Sant Antoni

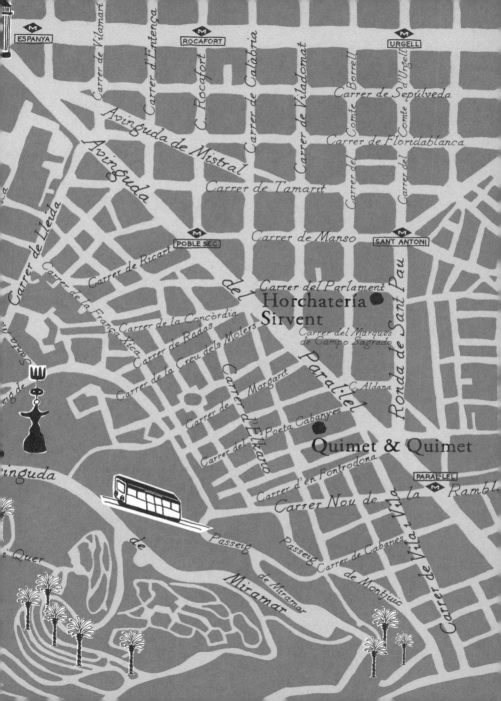

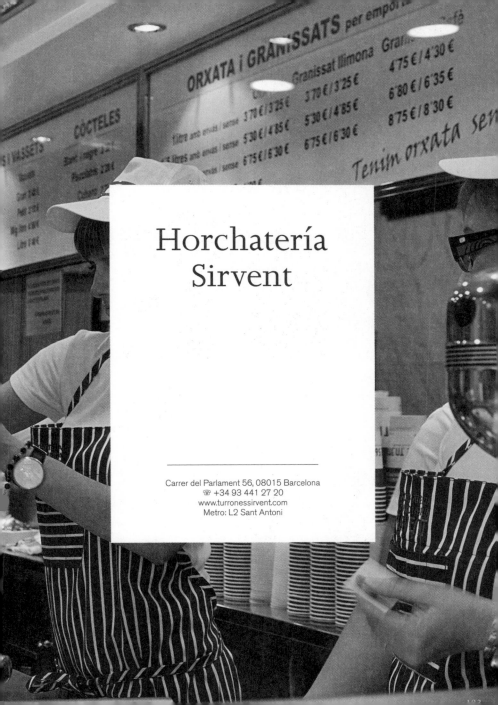

Horchatería Sirvent

Carrer del Parlament 56, 08015 Barcelona
☎ +34 93 441 27 20
www.turronessirvent.com
Metro: L2 Sant Antoni

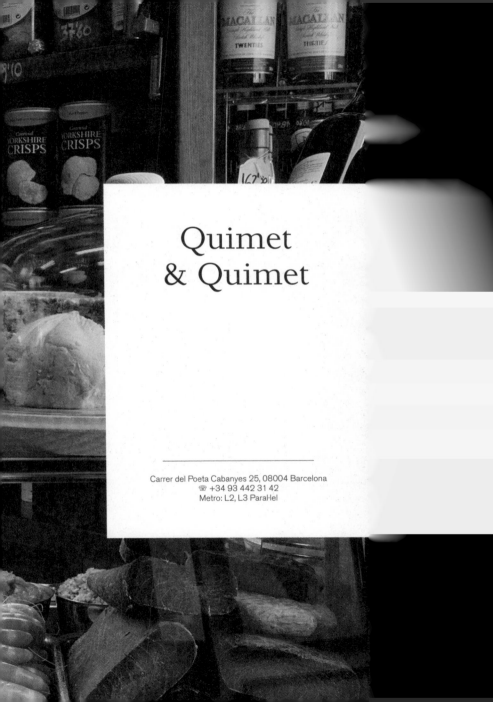

Quimet
& Quimet

Carrer del Poeta Cabanyes 25, 08004 Barcelona
☎ +34 93 442 31 42
Metro: L2, L3 Paral·lel

Horchatería Sirvent

Carrer del Parlament 56
08015 Barcelona
☎ +34 93 441 27 20
www.turronessirvent.com

pp. 182/183

Quimet & Quimet

Carrer del Poeta Cabanyes 25
08004 Barcelona
☎ +34 93 442 31 42

pp. 186/187

Traditional Milk & Nougat Bar
Interior: Nostalgic painted tiles

Open: Daily 10am–9pm | **X-Factor:** The "turrones" (nougat) |
Prices: Orxata from 3.25 €, turrones from 8.25 € (400 g).
In summer they make the best "orxata" in town – a refreshing
drink made out of earth almonds.

Öffnungszeiten: Täglich 10–21 Uhr | **X-Faktor:** Die
„turrones" (Nougat) | **Preise:** Orxata ab 3,25 €, Turrones ab
8,25 € (400 gr.).
Im Sommer wird hier die beste „orxata" der Stadt hergestellt
– ein erfrischender Drink aus Erdmandeln.

Horaires d'ouverture : Tous les jours 10h–21h | **Le « petit
plus » :** Les « turrones » (nougats) | **Prix :** Orxata à partir de
3,25 €, turrones à partir de 8,25 € (400 gr) | En été, on
prépare ici la meilleure « orxata » de la ville – une boisson
aux amandes de terre très rafraîchissante.

Traditional Bodega
Interior: With ancient advertising panels

Open: Tu–Sa 11am–4pm and 7–10.30pm; Su 11am–4pm |
X-Factor: The "pica pica" snacks | **Prices:** Wine from 1.50 €,
tapas from 1.75–11 €.
This long established family-run bar in the Poble Sec has an
outstanding selection of wines and cheeses.

Öffnungszeiten: Di–Sa 11–16 und 19–22.30, So 11–16
Uhr | **X-Faktor:** Die Häppchen „Pica Pica" | **Preise:** Wein ab
1,50 €, Tapas 1,75–11 €.
Diese alteingesessene, familiengeführte Bar im Poble Sec
bietet eine hervorragende Wein- und Käseauswahl.

Horaires d'ouverture : Mar–Sam 11h–16h et 19h–22h30,
Dim 11h–16h | **Le « petit plus » :** Les amuse-gueule « Pica
Pica » | **Prix :** Vin à partir de 1,50 €, tapas 1,75–11 €.
Cette vieille entreprise familiale au Poble Sec propose un
excellent choix de vins et de fromages.

© 2007 TASCHEN GmbH
Hohenzollernring 53, D-50672 Köln
www.taschen.com

Compilation, Editing & Layout
Angelika Taschen, Berlin

General Project Manager
Stephanie Bischoff, Cologne

Photos
Pep Escoda, Tarragona

Cover Illustration
Olaf Hajek, www.olafhajek.com

Maps
dieSachbearbeiter.*innen*, Berlin

Graphic Design
Eggers + Diaper, Berlin

Captions
Christiane Reiter, Hamburg

French Translation
Thérèse Chatelain-Südkamp, Cologne

English Translation
Pauline Cumbers, Frankfurt am Main

Lithograph Manager
Thomas Grell, Cologne

Printed in Italy
ISBN 978-3-8365-0053-1

To stay informed about upcoming TASCHEN titles, please request our
magazine at www.taschen.com/magazine or write to TASCHEN,
Hohenzollernring 53, D-50672 Cologne, Germany, contact@taschen.com,
Fax: +49 221 25 49 19. We will be happy to send you a free copy of our
magazine which is filled with information about all our books.